COR

TRU

THE CRYSTAL MOMENT

THE
CRYSTAL
MOMENT

Phyllis M. Jones

Kenwyn Publishers

Reprinted 2007

Published by
Kenwyn Publishers
Pen y Bont, Heol Sylen
Pontyberem, Carmarthenshire, SA15 5NW
Telephone: (01269) 870263
Fax: (01269) 870149

A CIP catalogue record for this book is
available from the British Library.

ISBN 0-9501891-8-9
978-0-9501891-8-5

Printed and bound in Wales by
Dinefwr Press Ltd.
Rawlings Road, Llandybie
Carmarthenshire, SA18 3YD

CONTENTS

PREFACE

Phyllis Jones is a passionate and nostalgic poet of this countryside, whether of Wales, where she has lived for many years, or her Cornish homeland; she observes intimately and acutely nature's multitudinous effects upon the scenes around her. 'Snow Blooms on the Cherry Tree' and 'Turning Leaves' are prime examples. This links with her awereness of Cornish mythology and life, seen in poems such as 'The Crystal Moment' and 'Holiday Aunt'; it also branches into Celtic Welsh mythology, present in 'Saint Non . . . Queen of Cornwall' and 'Still Life' among others. Her sense of the past and its legacy of sorrow and tragedy are sharply conveyed in poems such as 'The Front of the Church is Empty', 'November Light' and 'A Last Appraisal'.

Here is a collection to be savoured, and enjoyed over and over again. It is the fruits of a life, deeply felt and presented with great sensitivity for us all to experience.

Donald R. Rawe

ACKNOWLEDGEMENTS

Country Quest.
Anglo Welsh Review.
Cornish Review.
Cornish Scene.
The Baner, Cornwall.
Llanelli Miscellany.
The Bells of Truro.

THE CRYSTAL MOMENT

Each pebble jewelled the sea-bed, with harbour steps
Smoothed into stairs; carpeted in green, drowned weed
The water was melted crystal
So that to enter was to know the sparkling minute
Would be remembered once again
When age would consider sensual yesterdays.

I thought as I lay in the sea's lapping embrace,
Even in the shallow greenness of my years,
Of the time when all this transparency would cloud;

I thought with misted, time-distanced vision
And for my squandered innocence shed tears;

But the moment passed when the plunging body
Split the lighted depths and scattered foam.

CUSTOMS QUAY

Our quay rises two stones above the tide,
Fluid brown puppets
In ragged costume, convulse
In young rhythms . . . small splashes
Spray stone-flags and the curious;
Toes curl through weed and gull's droppings.

They dive and between they roost
Under anchor ropes like salted pigeons;

Joe stands by his boat, oak-faced and he waits
While the toffs decide
(he hopes before weather breaks)
round to Percuil or across,
it is the same to him . . . last year
next year and nothing changes;

only the faces of children.

Spring light floods stable
mare washes her tender foal
Life will stain bright straw

LATE EVENING
ON THE SHORE

Between the dunes and where the ebb runs still,
Here, where curved tide-line and dry sand converge,
Sea's limp debris and shoreline's soapy spill,
Haze of the day and evening's breath now merge
Into the sensuous embrace of wind,
A sun pervades the new created mists
and feet on wet sand stamp a joyful print:
with old ingredients, memories persist,
failures, lost chances and frail human hope
enhanced in twilight seem now a fearsome force,
all doubt must shadow ability to cope;
but bright these thoughts, now drawn from source,
this mollifying evening, past regrets assuage.

smoke spirals through light
its message from hidden flames
blue wreaths for grieving

CRY OF THE WHITE BUCCA

Each night I watch
from my hollow cavern
on the shore at Porthangwartha

nights when the moon's sorcery
changes Black Rock into a silver seal;
and a girl under her woven shawl

waits by the inexorable tide-line
for the cry of her man in the sea wind.

and I heard her lover's cry from glassy depths
behind white spume curtains.

I saw the girl's head tilt towards
the sound of the man's voice
and her hand touched her belly

I knew the child turned inside her
as she stood alone on the shingle

each night she waits,
her feet entwine and join
they sink into the tide-stirred sand

and on nights when the wind comes from the south
the sea horse springs from the breakers

plunges into a mating dance
bows a plumed head and nudges
her body with wide, breathing nostrils

and the cry will be thin and high
from the glass of dark water behind wild spume.

I was there on the moonlit night
of her vigil in the seventh month of her bearing,

the sea horse sprang from the tossing spray
and the south wind sounded and the man's cry
was loud as it echoed in the wind.

the sea green weed on the rocks
was hay and the shore was a plain
of grass and the sea horse

danced and pranced around the girl
whose stomach was high in her ninth month
and the shells on the rocks were lichens;

the sea threw tempestuous waves,
then they were still like clovered cliffs;

so the girl in her fishnet caul
rode the sea horse which was white as spray,
filled with the wind, they leapt

through clovered cliffs towards glassy depths,
the sough of the wind was in the man's voice.

the wind then ceased its moan
and the splintered sea merged,
it foamed towards the shore

the green plain once more was sand.
I am alone watching a glassy sea,
Black Rock floats on liquid silver.

DECEMBER IN GOWER

I have stared past the grey shallows
Of your eyes more times than I shall count
And heard the sounding of your voice
Break on tide line.

I have seen your lips curl like fragments
Of burnt paper, when a smile dies,
And felt the searing silence
Of your anger

I have felt freezing of a lover's breath
Sting like arctic flakes in a North wind
And felt entwining limbs turn numb . . .
When love is ice.

*Rain mist sweeps the field
at noon wind drives it faster
now is December*

THE FRONT OF THE CHURCH IS EMPTY

This pew was given by Williams
He was a big man for the church
And dead long since.

His children work in England
He invested in their learning
They won't return

No one ever sits in this seat
Because of respect for Williams
Sit further back

Jones, high street, gave us this pew,
The only thing he ever gave;
He died counting:

Glad to escape his wife married
Went with her children to England
They won't return

No one ever sits in this pew
Out of respect for Mr. Jones
Sit further back.

BANK HOLIDAY SENSES

Did you ever think that a seagulls' cry
Blending with a child's shrill laughter
Is a sound which smells of salt?

Sound receding into blue acoustics
Within the rocks, forms part of a clear
Orchestra which plays a high, ozonic note

And sings through a summer wind.

When you hear the impregnated sound
Wherever you are, you will feel grains
Of sand, warm where you sit

Taste grit in bank holiday food.

As you lean or loll against the stone hollow
Staked out with towels and striped gear,
Cost of the lease for the day;

If you close your eyes you will imagine
Once more, a swaying sand ballet . . .
Ice-cream and drinks held high on a tray,

Sugar lumps and steaming.

You will taste hot tea before it is poured
See those salt-crusted bodies spread
To become tanned by the sun.

If you run once more down to the shore
Step through foam as soap drains the tide,
Wonder as waves wash lace over prints

Of bare feet, dappling and smoothing

And smoothing and smoothing.
Draining away the proof of the day.

JANUARY LOVE

The beach is more white
In thin light and your steps
Snap through the web of frost
Woven last night.

Shivering we walk
On a tin shore and dawn
Splinters the brittle night
In winter shreds.

Bitter waves recede
Chilled by glacial shale,
Split twigs, strewn, drift into
A flimsy grave.

GERIATRIC WARD

Those hooks, flashing like talons,
We watched on bitter risings
When buses, grating from early depot,
Shook thin walls and threatened
The fragile window.

Each morning your pointed face,
Too young, was pale in pinched light:
Your teeth chattered, though you smiled
And fastened corset with icy hands.
We saw your cruel dawns.

How you heaved your soft body
Within confining straits
And how you brushed away
The dark, wasteful luxury of hair:
This was your pattern.

Making too dark the fabric,
Lit only by subtle stabbing gleams
Like laughter over our small triumphs
And crooning sounds of comfort
Over our failures.

Now your inert flesh, harnessed
By their careless hands is left;
An awkward monument to living:
Yet your grey eyes look into ours,
Seeking amusement.

Is it the smell of fresh urine:
Or your lying in flannel gown
With dark hair uncombed,
Which makes me remember
Those remorseless mornings?

DEATH IN A FARM KITCHEN

Old May, farm wife lay
A hulk, much seasoned,
Storm-scored;
Vital channels drain
On coarse bed

Brawny arms of rough sons
Strain to tilt the bulk
And daughters sigh;

Un-thoughtful spawn
This field of pity
Is another's land

Now May must lie
Disarmed and un-taut
To wonder

How long before she leaves
Her abject brood, subdued
Around her,
Withholding stretched hand,
Staying the gentle word?

HOLIDAY AUNT

I stole the Springtime
You turned and I crept into your warm kitchen
Carried laughter outwards and stored
Those vibrant fragments of your life
Along the shallows of my mind.

The seaweed on Castle beach crunched
under our bare feet and cool evening sand
fell into soft piles. You gossiped into darkness,
nights when a generous moon spilled
silver in the sea. We followed you,
ran circles, our leapings
a wild dance to the music of your voice.

I took your Summers
You toiled over a stove making pasties for strangers
Who sat on best chairs, looking at glass chimers
And horses of chained clome.
I gave a child's brown body and sand
From my toes sprinkled your floor.

I robbed you of autumn
Though you stayed rich for Falmouth air was sharp
and the Channel as blue as Summer.
The narrow rain-swept streets became our own.

All through the seasons
Your stories wove an enchanted novel of your life,
I kept the winter
Taking into my heart the sound of a Bechstein piano

Tuned into Christmas. Smells of goose, frozen sand
And seaweed mixed in a memory.

I can unlock my childhood,
Revel over stolen treasures;
Hands, frail and roughened
Trace their lost shapes.

THE BROWN SEA

As I walk towards the brown sea
At the edge, sometime, of this brown sand
I am the shadow of the one thing moving
In a wheeling disc horizon. If I look back
Over the flat track towards lost dunes
I cannot see the sharp grass growing;
Once I knew it was there,
Green and trapping the western wind;
I ran singing over dry sand
And reaching out could lock fingers
In crumbling cliff shale,
I knew if I turned towards you
Then would be your smile.

But I walk towards the brown sea
At the edge sometime, of this brown sand.

MORNING AT CARLYN

Pale light wakens a city
cautious, slanting upwards;
before it unwraps windows and doors;
these merchant people
allow the day's sounds full value,
morning highlights the viaduct

as it trails into foliage,
the first rattling encounter
with another world;

so soon mist dissolves
sleepy town vibrates
a train whistles and
crawls from the city.

Sunlight scratches with one finger
a mist from a filmed panorama
stirs market senses.

Traffic winds over shifting roads
past places once green like Newham
or Idless, snakes past giant hoardings
searching secrets from the Celtic West

Step from this noisy current
into past dereliction
look at new mystery;
Old monuments . . . yes . . . even Engine houses
are ethereal in moonlight
shattered by broken bricks.

Grass covers old scars
and walls protect like a carved tombstone
here scrubland is a garden
wilderness freed points the way
to silence.

There goes the London train
over valley, whistling
into foliage and the hanging mist.

Welcome back cold air
four swallows hang on the line
their moment has gone

THOUGHTS INSTILLED

He called the Canary Kruger
I never understood;
he mentioned often 'Old Bill'
he joked if we rebelled
'If you can find a better 'ole'

and two shell cases . . . shining brass
stayed on the mantelpiece;
one held a jagged artifice, his
shrapnel . . . he touched with deferential hand
tracing a contour; touching the ragged edge.

At times his eyes looked inwards

he saw a place which he had known
facial lines grew taut
we knew that in this maze
of mind some spectres haunted still . . .
of these he could not speak.

Yet in the silence of a November's day
shared by the men who knew
we heard some anguished heart's beat
tuned to an unheard memory . . .
concentrated thought . . .yet separate.

SAIL BOATS AND MACKEREL

Under rubble
the thin whisper of her life
laments against new walls.

She walks on lopsided stairs
and her grey rustle is heard
through the stark bedroom;
the leaning windows are open to salt black
stabbed by starlight,
or voices, pealing across water.

She bustles through the lurching cottage
in the cornered room
we knew in winter when thick baize
covered the spying window.

She opens the street door
into a stone passage
scented with new bread and fresh mackerel.

Her whispers are heard
more clearly in the kitchen
against a small orchestra;
made up of singing kettles and gossip,
the soft roaring as wreck wood burns,
the insistent beat of laughter.

I am the child who scrabbles
over boats at low tide

like a sand-fly;
I call through a maze of anchors;
my brown legs, spindling out of jeans,
leap in the drumming madness
of a primal furry dance.

The rounded sea walls are warmed
by sun; still they thrust
wide shoulders against sea spray.
These stones are mine
and all the years when I trapped dreams.

Dust from debris
clings round his sturdy ghost
and the mackerel wind sweeps through;
a door bangs.
the sawing door
pushes life through bent walls
and his voice sings once more
From sail boats past Black Rock.

A lorn spirit in dark jersey
rolls through the bunch-backed passage;
rocks up the swaying hill;
swings back, touches more gently
the walled road with trailing
Clematis over white-washed villas
on Castle Drive where shrubs breathe
perfume through salt and there are glimpses
of water, like chips of sapphire.

He is the pale evening harbour;
or the raucous concertina on the Quay;
beer in 'the Ship' on Regatta Day;
his rough presence
Is felt in the blue, chopped dawn.

Grouped on a sea canvas
the ballet of tall ships return;
sail colours slash grey water
sunlight on stone mellows 'Place',
as candle glow flatters age,
burnishing with flame;
making more beautiful.

The dark waters stir slowly
below St. Just In Roseland;
the old bell measures seasons;
how many times at midnight
they will both listen, wondering,
'Is the sea lilting still
between the rolling fields?'

A CHILD SENSES THE WIND

At first it was firelight,
Sparking in eyes . . . a flame,
Flash of crimson in skirt,
Whirling, almost unseen;
The minute passing quickly,
Too quickly . . . slow down my gipsy,
Time for your laughter
To echo and rekindle
Memories, smouldering.

To have what I had,
Some day will have
What I have . . . slow down
My gipsy . . . know joy.

Once there flames
And now a wind tears
At tatters, swift streaming
From young shoulders,
Those little tags which
Flew towards happiness
(and frightened cows)
a breeze tugging at life.

Whirling gipsy skirt,
Flying bright ribbons
That colour the wind

FALLING LEAVES

Those thoughts forever drifting
Winged sycamore
Which brushes autumn earth:

Dreams ensnared,

Brief words entrusted
To buff, deceptive envelope
Teasing the mind

As debris piles on new mounds,
Mulch, time softened
So subtly ferments;

Fragments of joy or hurt
Will layer as leaves float
Sadly, to lie in woodland;

It is I who am shorn.

TO A FISHERMAN

The rocks all mourned him;
Grouped at the shoreline
They gathered the lacing foam;
'This is his shroud,' they said

the gulls were screaming,
keeners, their wailing
drowned the lamenting wind:
'We'll sing his dirge,' they said.

And the waves whispered,

'We have his secret,'
and on his sea bed soft he lies,
'We'll keep his soul,' they said.

let us drink fine wine
soft red glow in the afternoon
a whole world rosy

NOVEMBER LIGHT

I slip into your room, I do not speak,
Knowing my pity is so loud it
Stirs the filming dust and clenches
Your hand above the rumpled sheet.

Three crows, flat against a bowed branch
Keep watch, their noiselessness a threat,
And those flowerbeds in spring, once bright
With hope, now strewn with faded leaves,
Are paisley-patterned graves.

If I divined the shadows of November
Were brilliant with your dreams and
This present stillness in the sparkling
Silence off Pill Creek when
Alouetta's stuttering engine ceased,
The mournful crows might be gulls
Wheeling over Point, and we could
Share a smile . . . the bonfire's gleam,
The smell of gutted fish . . .
Like banners they were strung.

Do not draw the blind, you say,
It shuts out light, then in my mind I add,
November's light is measured,
And, as the sun stays skulking,
Waiting its chance to staunch the flowing day.

I watch you as you savour
Each piercing, dying ray.

THERE BUT FOR
THE GRACE OF GOD

Gwyneira in rags bought flowers today
Which bright amongst her boxes lay,
The boxes which festooned her arms;

Cardboard boxes and coloured flowers
And twining straw which jettisoned
From woollen cap with wisps of greying hair.

How old? Birthdays forgotten as childhood friends
Who peopled picnics, spread on golden lawns,
Always in summer, and grew to aliens.

Mad Maisie, Gwyneira and the cross old dame,
Fey Mother Morris who lived along the lane
And gathered wood as Gwyneira clutched her boxes.

The shrill deaf mute who screamed beside the shore
Across Tolverne and dabbed the boats with tar
Her garments torn as a tattered sky.

How wild the dreams of Mopus Jen
And mazed as stars as she slept sound
Beneath an upturned hull on shingled river strand.

And top-side-down as any in the land:
Then Joan is extra coy and feeds her bread
To cats and the donkey whose hybrid cry

Is heard at night by Vera who fed foxes:
Elusive these frail souls the world will never hold
As Gwyneira held her boxes.

I HELD A SEA STONE

It felt of living
Almost as if my own blood flowed
Between us, or, was it sun's memory,
Yellow lights in a rock pool
Where it had lain.

My craving urged me,
I reached under warm, sea-weeded
Water, curling my fingers
To grasp, a sensual action,
I drew it from sea bed;

And afterwards, as I slept
I held the living pebble;
Specks of rock quartz
Stabbed back sparks of sun
And there was heat in my hollow hand.

Now it lies in dark
Recesses my room,
A small sentinel, forgotten,
Except for glance, too apathetic,
My eyes gleam life's remnants.

Hands thin, without their curling strength
Reach out to touch and wonder
Why in seven centuries
Or seventy-seven times seven
My stone will be still young.

TURNING LEAVES

I had written
of new thoughts like silver willow buds
ready to burst into life with the Spring,
singing and warm, touching, tentative
as tendrils curling;
dreams in the drenched leaf-moulded soil
were not credible.

I had written
of new boundaries with boulders strewn
to be rolled or pushed with braced sinews
strong in ambition; straining to attain
as a branch stretches, holding;
dreams in the growing summer fields
may be realised.

I shall write now
of evening skies tinged with bruising mauve
laced with red, veining stains, more lovely
than past, wistful mind remembers . . . shadows
so many, deepen and frost creeps, edging nearer;
there is darkness, quick in the evening,
there is darkness.

Autumn and the word
sharpens each day with regret
last colours fade.

SNOW BLOOMS
ON THE CHERRY TREE

On winter tree
A pruned spray traces the small light;
Planed patterns cross the low sun.
Only the bark's gloss matches sheen
On past blossoms.

Austere branches
Arch like a cat's claw.
Jet slanting over iced furrow,
Cruel scimitar, rounding earth
Hard like anthracite.

Or moon-softened
In phosphorescent light,
Which deceives like the catalectic line;
Each tendril bearing
A frozen star.

The lacing bough
Stark like starvation
Is a scar on the staring sky;
Or fragile bone
Picked by Buzzard on bleached earth.

Cherry tree in winter!
No green could make more delicate.

THE SCENE

Eyes glitter like lakes
Neon-lit in Woolworth glasses
Quick fingers dip
Among the vol-au-vents
And glib words
Make longed for social passes

Cheese impaled, angelica caught
On cocktail sticks in taut rows;
Minute forests, tobacco fogged
A stockade
Fencing emotions
Only breaking with charmed words

Eyes then are remote
Smudged by thought, lost moments,
Adolescent memories
Which strip the careful poise
From a face now vulnerable
As if a door had slammed

THE ALDER TREE

Only the rowan and ragged oak
Watch as my thin branch
Bends and rain deepens my marshy bed

I lean as reeds arrow the path
Of the wind which knives
On Sylen and whines
Towards the Channel

I am unsung though my roots hold firm
The uplands. Alone
I saw the mountain sink
And Sylen stones grow white

There is an owl's cry
Before dawn sound drawn from woods;
Who is the hunted?

The catkin drips light
a lantern over stream
illuminating

STILL LIFE

(Comment on a stone statue 'Mare and Foal' created by an unknown Celt)

He shaped living into stone and stone
Shaped living. Nothing changes not
When the earth sings and the kindling sperm
Stabs into life when there is nothing

Was it morning when he looked,
With grass wet after rain: wind driving cloud
Through early skies?

Before time . . . before time we knew
One man looked over his green world;
He saw the moment he would carve
Out of time . . . to blend all time.

The beginning was primal conflict

Stallion circles his springing kingdom
Snorting fierce fervour, bears down
Would be usurper; thrashing air,
They entangled and leapt together, arching;
Muscles rippled, silk waving

Ritual before a female power.

The lit eyes, darkly, assure fulfilment:
In the end and the beginning
She is the source of life,
Tranquil as she crops:

One infiltration and a lazer flame;
One time, one revelation, one orgasm,
And so the slow gestation . . . Miracle
Of birth

Dance colt over dappled grass with flaming coat,
Catching sun-fire, your life seizing scents
Of springtime, leaping
As wind chases rain.

Slow . . . so slow the placid milky flow;
Warm udders full, the song of life she knows
Is soft breathing and a song of green land;
Thundering, whinnying sounds of the herd.

This fragment of life caught in time;
Milk and the foal . . . milk-white the mare,
Balance of life in timeless scales.

Was it morning when he looked,
With grass wet after rain, wind driving cloud
Through early skies?

CHILD OF THE PEATLANDS

Once near the quagmire as a child
Close to the fluting reeds I crawled
And I laughed in Winter

Now if I look outside
Where people team, writhing,
I will miss the scent
Of sedge sweet, misty air;
I must read about herbs,
Lavender and mint and must recall
The green freshness of parsley;

For in my island I remember,

Lancing reeds in rows point upwards
To a watery sun;
The black moss menaces;

There are generals
Who record their wars
And there are warnings
Brought by fugitives from countries
Intimidated:
I can pity safely
When you are gone:

Now nothing matters.

Clouds engrave darkened water
The slim reeds sway
And sadly moor-hens call.

I can remember love
In words, now erotic,
Changed from Bard's intent, I forget
café tables or eyes locking
through cigarette smoke
or how the window framed
another world;

gone is your loving

Though reeds still scent marshes
They are far away
Across lanes of concrete;

Here without moving
I recollect green sabres,
Sibilant, clashing secrets,
As wind wallows through fen:
When I hear the damped
Low cadences will sound
So solitary:

Inside these pages there is longing.

I shall find my strength
Through vellum and morocco
In all life catalogued:
I shall be scorched or bled
And shall cry pulped tears,
According to the word.

OUR MORASS

We are the rushes
Waving in wasteland
We are shadowed swamps
Beyond reclaim

Sweep us with wind
Flatten us
We shall return

Swept by the sun,
Cloud dappled,
Wind rippled,
We fringe the stream

Close woven green:

Entangling the glow,
Reeds are moon-steeled,
Glittering stalks
like bayonets,
blinding . . .

then in rushlike-rusting
quagmired beds of cunning,
innocence drowns

stalks of disillusion,
hollowed stems
out-thrust from marsh,
whispering en masse
involved in our morass;

hollowed stem,
conveyed despair;
in fluting cries,
pining for help
from all we condemn.

Drained of all light
Truth is stark
Yet truth remains.

We are the rushes;
Waving in wasteland;
We are shadowed swamps
Beyond reclaim.

Past two lunar months
Groomed is the garden and sweet
All birds feed their young

PASSERS BY

Over red marshes between the hills
Are tracks where ancients roved
And on the low ridge, foliage spring
Where I buried you, my love

They say I am crazed because I stand
In the doorway of my earth house
And sing songs in the evening:
I sing because summer comes.
Though the moors lie in their purple shrouds
And Bumble Bees drone their mourning,
In tenuous night mist the memory of winter
Drowns in a growing scent;
I watch the white, spraying flock make carpets
Edged by the yellow gorse.

I sing because the taste of Whinberries
Is bitter and sweet the scent of wild mint:
My thoughts leap from the twilight
As I sing with the Skylark singing.

They walk past my earth house
To the mound . . . he had grown tall;
He walked in old clothes as if he had to;
Her hair grew long which is good on a summer's day:
But with my darker sight I see her
When shrill winds cry and winter
Tangles her hair: I see him bringing in rushes
As you did, for mending the roof . . . and the peat;

The rain bends his shoulders;
They touch the blue, covering heather
And look at each other, laughing;
They wonder as they try to hold the minute
And wind their arms together.

Who picked the furze and gathered the peat?
Who rolled back the rain cloud?
Is that a sigh or the wind from curved hillock
Where you lie in your burial ground?
I sing in the evening but they have passed me:

The Skylark joins in my song.

*There is the black earth
tuned again by the man's fork
Spring has its new smell*

MOUNTAIN SILENCE

I sit, halfway through time,
in its grained, glacier cradle
listening in the carved silence;
I strain to hear
forgotten forest whispering;
echoes of Merlin or a threat,
the vibration, drumming
from some exploring car,
not yet factory assembled.

But the faded, mountain-grey turf
drinks every sound
except the soft, tearing reed-wind
and a pistol crack
 which is the wash of lake water.

BETRAYAL

Boulders lay aeonian,
stemmed in soil and mobilised
to bruise; they were his force,

dormant in the mountain and were his own,
as were wide trees and
the wind was on his side.

> 'Words are our weapons' others said
> honed by envy
> and greed-sharpened,
> flint arrows to menace,
> 'We shall take you from your hill.'

They skivered his world with smiles.

His life persisted in the sheen
on bent grass and his keening
was recognised by reeds;

chuntering in gullies
was echoed in the lowing
of his bewildered herd and in
the snuffling of his calves.

GIRL PICKING BLACKBERRIES

Nia . . . did you need
a sombre hat to hide
a pale expression, enigmatic?
your smile disguising,
letting us not through.

this is the moment
to lighten shadows,
when all the young
who love the summer
run through the waves
and savour blackberries.

cram down the clown's hat
if life might seem too dazzling,
but I would tilt the brim
and scan the stretching meadow.

Even the sun which sets each night
dips tentatively into the next
confusion and those
of all the days ensuing.

MEETING A CONTEMPORARY

My yesterday thoughts . . .
too many for one day's page,
swallows and earth and a lost purse;
this old lady . . . ten years older than
myself, both fighting years, we said
in our brief conversation . . . why and now
and for what?

I thought of a boy with youth
all energy who half mowed the bank
and threw weeds in the river, not caring,
and how I dug the earth, feeling
the brown, crumbly tilth and
knowing life. And Danny,
no idea, pulling an easy weed and then
his cigarette papers . . . his energy spent
in rolling fingers and the drawing
in of smoke. Oh, how we old ones spoke.

I thought of Gwyn and how my debt
to him was paid through my small labours . . .

so many generations and mutations and
strangely less to be seen . . . frailty reduces
value of weeks and months
less is seen and more forgotten.

contempt is undeserved.

Tomorrow I
shall fork the yellow straw to bed
the mares and draw the hay
to racks and pull the Rosebay Willow.

SAINT NON . . .
QUEEN OF CORNWALL

Mother of Saint David

This is my seat . . . eisteddfa:
I look westwards
Through wide and ancient oaks
Searching our Cornish light

Translucent

I smell wet lands and salt
And feel sea spray
If my eyes close and, for a while
Passion fades

Love of my Cornish world
And taste of power . . . woman's power . . .
The gentle mare or placid cow
Who crops the soil
Which men have stained with blood.

On Eisteddfa's slope I gaze
Towards the west:
I dream and live through hours
When touch and flesh began . . .
The mazing stream which carried
Saints and kings and moved
The mounds of fate

Yet dry my own smooth child!

Destiny fulfilled . . . his passion too austere
The waterman . . . the saint for Wales

Ironic!

Stones which form as cushions
To my back as when I lean
In my strong seat and let my mind
Fly to Cornish moors or over
Coves in Brittany are not as hard
As David's dreams.

Yet he will have his day made bright
With daffodils . . . children will sing
And feasting bring
His desiccated destiny to mind

Besides the Cornish ocean in
A dreaming vision as I sit
Will rivers fierce as rape
Or flowing sweet on lovers' bed
Forever flood.

My soul is found on Celtic wind
In depths of wells and sometime
Be enclosed by Llannon's own church walls.

ON THE HILL

Ynysteddfyn is built in the wind
Hunched on a mattress of peat
The windows watch seven counties
From Brecon to Rhossili. But the eyes
Of Will and Jack regard the hill road,
Rest on shorn grass in a summer barn,
See the silky flanks of Welsh Blacks,
Razor spines cutting Winter storm
And cleaving a way through seasons.

Truculent, the wind rampages,
Strums through wires and fined branches,
Skirls over Sylen
And knives through the bones of the mountain;
See how white the thinning grass,
How thick the foliage
Where whin masses on the ridge,
And feel how warm the trough which follows,
Like a summer bower.

Only the old ones know
Where the red kiosk stood,
a lighthouse on Sylen,
beaconing thick-walled holdings
the breeches-buoy for last aid,
undertaker or knackers' yard;
progress stepped on time and stripped this spot
but the kiosk and our stone-walled chapel
are still recalled . . . by the old ones.

Rampaging, the wind
Strums through wires and fined branches,
Skirls over Sylen;
Blows from Brecon to Rhossili and, still
Eyes of two brothers see the mountain,
Eyes rest on summer grass they piled in barn;
Wondering as Welsh Blacks
Seem rooted in peat lands,
Enduring as the Genie of the hill.

now hang golden chains
June will lighten hedgerow
brightening summer

THE SOUND OF REBELLION

A stone stays on the hillside
flat and glossed blue-white,
scoured by years and weather,
stroke patterns and dents . . . printed,
maybe, by boulders prised from peat bed,
now locked in the heart of a chimney;
this stone is a tablet, magnetic,
tenacious and sufficient.

Memory sees apple baskets in September
and Pen-y-bont set amongst pink blossom,
children trailed down hill past the bridge,
past the cottage where they took their fruit.

Roan cob struggles with market load
the lurching cart rattles through low cloud
young farmers dream of another world
which is no other world, reality is rain;
drained fields streaming into new tracks;
they think how tinkers threw lost children
for foxes, how a man sank through Bryndu mire;
they see nothing through slanting rain
and huddle under cloaks of sacking.

They came over paths now lost,
hidden in thicket or under stolen green,
riding on gambos

 or rough-hewed carts;
Sylen, then roomy, hosted their hundreds,

listened and stirred their grievance,
Rebecca's sons went back through the ways
they travelled, taking a sound of rebellion
which they knew would recede
behind the walls of the cow shed.

First Snowdrops were seen by the river
awakening in frost and, in summer
a new awareness . . . now Eve has the apple
recalls unspoilt moments when small hands
were filled with bright fruit, tasting of love.

Scent of hay fresh cut
fills the lane and evening
Each year is the same

'TWAS NEVER THUS

(Return journey to St. Agnes after eighty years)

Steep Stippy-Stappy
There was a space for sure
Steps which slipped
Towards white tips . . . sea waves were keen

Young minds felt shock
The world was rough
Sheep stood clean and still
There were fields lush green

And on the hill a child stares
Stepping across the top
Of Stippy-Stappy, she must see
Through space beside a hedge

Must touch – monster meh-ed and meh-ed
She would have fled

Then the beach with sand stained red
'from the mines' the old man said
'no one complains
our raddled tin remains'

then the market days were shrill
squealing pigs around the hill
fearful as man prepared to kill
'Oh steep Stippy-Stappy'

to assuage a yearn
I return in mind to sea and sun
Once was mine when life was fun
Stepping down steep Stippy-Stapp

no lane – a street, rough stones sharp
hurt tender feet and old bones creaked

now sea narcotic
and it is grey
straining surfers feign their play.

CHYSAUSTER

A yellow sign said 'Prehistoric Village'
Monument! Ministry of works
To share administration with elements?
(even now I can hear the boned hills
rock with laughter)
It pointed over stone stiles
Where flags, polished by feet
Bared soles; boots, leather-thonged
And our summer sandals stamped
A pattern back from the year of plastic.

Alone in the thrust of square slabs
I heard an echo of living,
Here, in the squatting wind-breaks
Men laughed and hunted and rough-hewed
Our present with blunt hands
Heeding their audacious star:
And here are the huts of an old settlement
Backs to the wester-wind,
Open doors facing a new sun each day
Always new!

Through drizzling centuries, on shoaly soil,
Green-grey lichen kilted granite,
Confirming the shadows.

SO SPOKE THE WEATHERMAN

Alone with words and weather
Syllables twine inside the mind
To link past thoughts

From radio a voice fails
To suppress its warning
'Severe weather over North and West'

fear . . . that means us

tomorrow I shall seek the word
surrealism I must comprehend
all implications

storm threatens, arrows on weather map
packed close as in the fields of Pontiers,
remind of death

mountain adds quota, floods form 'Oh the wind'
hail spatters the glass each pane becomes
too frail . . . I am alone

too old . . . with my 'familiar' . . . she cowers
finding furthest corner;
my bitch cannot know this black night

only her skin vibrates her hair stiffens
she shivers and ignores words
and my caress

with lamp, I found a way to light,
and, with the wind, my mind impels
my body towards stables . . . a whinney

soft muzzles welcome, seek frozen fingers
seeking fruit . . . the apple always tempts

their breath consoles.

NIGHT ASSAULT

October . . . and yesterday, when season's aging
Soaked the glut of blackberries,
Brought scarlet beads to holly
And hung rowan to flame against a lower sun;
The leaves, dying in still, slow-ebbing
Leapt with death-throw gestures
Into dance dreams
Fraught with myriad colours,
Vivid, to cling more surely,
Surely, reds and rusts and orange yellows
Must deflect this autumn blight.

From deep across the frontier folds of night,
Sounds of aggressive wind-strength
Sweeping wet, smoked mist from left fields,
Lonely, now the herd is sheltered.
No gusts, terrier tugging,
Just a distant moaning threat,
Insistent, warning, before morning,
That all the brilliant fire
Of reds and rusts and orange yellow
Will lie dormant,
Bereaving trees to pattern winter light.

OAK TREE MID-FIELD

Animals sprawled between roots,
Spread feet of Dinosaurs, formed
Homes in clefts, each wall
To ward all winds

Shadows crossed grew longer
With years, natures energy
Made certain branches move with seasons

Leaves misting in Spring
Sheltering life in summer
Shielding in Winter

From rain and sun rays
Each leaf a tender parent
Protects its own

When at dawn I searched
Crossing land for latest foal,
So senses told, it would be born,
I knew the tree could tell

This is her private time
She will share one moment
Before gathering her new-light form
Throwing high her head so breeze

Teases the mane into new patterns,
Floating 'come foal and follow'
Sweeping . . . a command yet barring
All who would make claim.

SEVEN AGES OF WOMAN

Shall I love seven times
Remembering my first love,
Seven times seven years past?

Then twice I loved, I thought that love could last;
So many doubts came with acceptance
When your love I returned . . . my third,

Quite justified. Oh how I yearned!
Such is experience. I learned one must be tough.
I spurned the fourth . . . thought I had loved enough.

The one who got away. I was a fool.
No memories of kisses, warm or cool,
No caresses, still to shiver as I drool

(not in my dotage quite) I recall the next,
the fifth, I should know him well,
we walked through many paths, entwined,

beginning in the aisle, we watched
the same suns rise; rode the same tide;
I thought I would have died

When he walked away, treading the leaf-strewn path
We both had shared: I never would have dared
To take the sixth, you understand,

I had not planned to be unfaithful,
But life is short without a charmed escort,
No one to court and bring those feline thoughts
    Or break a heart if two must part . . .
    Oh . . . shall I love seven times!

THE GRASS HAS
NOT YET GROWN

Not while I stand
with each muscle tensed
against the stone squeeze, is the drift
in its emptiness
forsaken.

Not if I hear
deep whispers, feel pulsing
the compressors and fans
of the great cutter;
and am able still
to tremble.

Not while I sense
the earth sigh in
the thin dawn
as the warm mandrel
splits the East and
my lips pale
will my dark battle ground
be lonely.

Only when the grass has grown
I will hear echoes in stone,
scattered in last pewkings;
of moaning or feet crunching and
the sound of gaunt laughter
in black corridors.

CARNIVAL IN HIGH STREET

Lines of bunting stream across the road
low flying, touching tops of lorries
taking coal, and, thinking of
past ceremonies, old men lean
against their doorways, oak-weathered
pathways to sky.

Slanting on hill, self-consciously,
cars park, but women gossip still
with words thrown backwards
as they hurry through afternoons,
mornings are empty always, and nights
are kept for grief

except when coloured flags, swinging,
link window frames . . . ribbons flowing
Strands outstretch from Maypole,
our winding tower, entwining patterns,
criss-crossing and entangling,
we celebrate

and sacrifice with pagan laughter.
Old ties renew, like memories
of High Street when it was filled
with young men and people leant
against their doorways
as they do now.

THREE TIMES THE BELL RINGS

Three bells. The cage clangs open,
slides shut and you are laid,
still shaking shale dust
upon the pit head floor and now
with straggling tenderness
bearers straighten backs and breathe.
You smile

It is the smile I need as
from the stretcher, strapped
tight by belts, glossed by wear
and in torn blankets wrapped;
untidy, tough cocoon!
I meet your eyes.

You grasp the cigarette and tea,
a proffered canteen cup,
grimy from coal-seamed hands;
its stain not lessening,
the slaking, sweetness of the drink,
sluices the dusty taste of dark.

Not less the warm anxiety of men
but pity, thinned with guilt,
knowing the odds, by reason of the
stone and how it closely missed
ourselves, must now be less.

The smile which shows
when your turn came you did not fail . . .
the smile you give we need.

THE MACABRE WINDERMAN

In the Winding Tower
He laughs and releases power;
He waits.

A cage filled with darkness
Clangs into day
A door tolls and dust
Muffles lusty tramping;

Dust into dust!

Laughing into daylight
And new sadness
He catches sorrow by the hand,
Watching;

What entertainment,
This melancholy carnival;
Dead faces move like balloons
Through springtime.

BLACK HARVEST

We found a strength
Power to bargain against men
Who operate;
There was at last a dignity,
A canopy
Which sheltered and we thought we knew,
Until we grew.

The shaft which led
Rutting hollows, deep and cutting
Roots exchanging
These for nothing, though we thought
Our labour bought
Was fair exchange. It's true we know
The price was low.

There was a bond
Around, to knot a cord which bound;
The world was ours,
The tunnels and the dark, the blood
Was ours. Too late
To find that no one coveted
Our splendid stock.

Nothing is left,
Not the green country . . . honey-combed;
An empty pit;
Black rubble scattered in pewkings;
A miner stripped
More naked than the day we bent
In the dark heat.

ON A GOOD DAY

This is a good day
thoughts leap. I know
whichever fence is built
or ditch laid . . .
safe landing
footsteps have new force
wrong . . . it is the old force,
when days were long
unshackled, I would turn
from confines of this room
towards bright faces,
still remembered.
I would talk
and talk and hold my own
and argue, to hear another
and to laugh. I have the power
if there was only
someone there.

THE LAST ECHO FADES

As I grope in the stifling vault
My bone and brain attack;
Shaking the earth, making this sound
Assault the dark.

My split-tongued spirit
Mute, like a mountain gnome,
With mandrel, flinting words
Creates a stone-fire discontent:

My hands are supplementary,
Not to fooled senses
But to the jolting tool
Pick or axe and now the cutter,
Are accessories to desecration

      And my eyes wrap round light,
      Blind in the first iridescence
      On my emergence, fine dusted:

Forced inside me is a fury
As if the green translucence
Is but more of God's unequal
Allocation.

Even the seeds squandered in easy love
Will not create the soul and child,
Not my own! Only a quick
Impression, fading like life itself.

When last ripples smooth, my broad grave
Will never be my creation;

And the perpetual stars,
My legacy, struck in the gloomy mint,
Will not illuminate
Mixed stone and ash.

DYLAN AND DECEMBER

Down tawny paths, littered from boned branches
Sunless in the dark December tea time
A ball bounced in Cwmdonkin Park

And sounded against the wet hill, hollow,
Echoing memory of scattered time

Kicked leather through the low, trapped sky still thuds
Boots parting dishevelled leaves on soaked paths
Trudge in wasteful pleasure

A boy's shout, sad, like the cawing rook's finale
Is sharp in the chilled afternoon and lonely
Words, multi-patterned, freeze those days, this day

THE CHAIN

This was our walk
past stream and cottage
where a grass-way led
to the quarry's broken face;
we held the chain,
I remember its strength; a trust
in our young bodies
as we swung.

Now as I dream
inside my ring of years
I make my own return;
but the path left no trace
and rain planed the quarry's face
the quarry is worn by wind . . .
no one could swing
on the rusty chain.

SONG OF THE HILL

(To the folk tune of Bessie Watson)

Oh how I need our Sylen hill
The open stretches where I feel
The breath of freedom on my skin
The sweep of stringent sun and wind.

I walk through fog and drizzling rain
Pick whinberries wild in Penlwyn Lane

I see the Rosebay dip and sway
A swirl of field-fares as they play;

If winds can take and lift my love
Like buzzards ride the sky above
Why should those turbines sweep away
The memory of Rebecca's day.

Why should our skyline and our space,
Our wilderness be so defaced
Welsh Blacks whose sharp and arrowed lines
Etched the horizons with their spines.

And when the mountain's mood is grey
Those times I know love may not stay
I wonder why the bright seas drain
And colour fades in mist again

If winds can take and lift my love
Like Buzzards ride the sky above
Why should those turbines sweep away
The memory of Rebecca's day

NOSTALGIA (SW)

Through wet lanes and hedges
Smelling of roots and earth,
Generations of plants,
The long-tongued fern licked frost
And snow scattered the path;

here the ford as I knew;
cars splashed and smug drivers
savoured novelty,
such quaintness, so unspoilt the air
and people . . . like peasants still!

And the hill,
Easy for these powered wheels;
I saw a pony, bowing under market load,
Trudging the track now called a road.

On river banks linked by small craft
Stretching like bracelets the span;
Through cold sunlight I saw
A collection of steeled strength,
Iron grey, forbidding solid might

Remnants of another decade
Too strong for scrap.

Time to leave . . . to leave . . .
To leave;
To wonder about roots
Twining down to twist through different soils;

Growing deeper,
Flower-heads scorched by sun;
Leaves saturated in dew;
Plants, mysterious in moonlight:
Only the open sky above;
No closeness here. Grow down; grow down
Return . . . return . . . return,
Seek the seeds remembered warmth.

CHRISTMAS RETURN

Come round the Christmas table, find a seat!
Let's taste the roasted bird with festal flair;
Tales and family lore are due for a repeat;

Trimmed holly puddings and mince pies to eat,
Then bird demolished, most of bones laid bare;
Come round the Christmas table, find a seat!

We watch the faces strain as in-laws meet,
Though laughter warms the feast of too rich fare,
Tales and family lore are due for a repeat

Bright Christmases past recalled as a treat,
Will never to this laboured meal compare;
Come round the Christmas table, find a seat!

Memories revived will strive the years to beat;
Aunt Flo exaggerates as much as she will dare;
Tales and family lore are due for a repeat.

Food and excess, frail stomachs will defeat
A Rennie first, then sleep in favourite chair.
Come round the Christmas table, find a seat:
Tales and family lore are due for a repeat.

ACROSS THE TAMAR

Old hills, soft as night
Rise on either side, only
Now and then a filled copse
Breaks the pattern . . . familiar
When seen again.
Green . . . green. In winter's light
Forgotten green, for memory is blue
And hot like a summer sea.

Wet paths show under tall, boned trees
Which reach from sky to valley floor
Y shaped, the season's yield abandoned.
If I could trace my steps again,
Stirring torn leaves with polished shoe,
When I return.

The low sun sucked the sea's strength,
Black stripes across yellow light;
The thunderous, grey Atlantic
Was dark and bright, changing swiftly,
Catching the wind shadow:
I saw a long, high wave,
Turning and curling;
Hurling towards the shore:

    The cliffs were bared of summer smiles
    And this was home.

WINTER JOURNEY
TO THE SOUTH WEST

We rode past frosted waste,
Fields worn by Saturday football frays
Passing pools, industrial, yet silver,
Mirroring low cloud;
Through featherd heads of grass
Sun shone and lit the plain
Set in its own rusted filigree.

    Through back gardens of grey houses,
    Black, leaning sheds matching neighbours'
    Nondescript . . . vibrating
    We rocked towards the west:

Ice trapped floods around trees
In fields, un-shadowed, in the morning:
A frozen pattern spread through brakes,
Futile on the flat green.
Only the wide, slow river
Moved in corrugated blue and was warm
In fragile, winter hue.

    Inside the steam fug, eyelids
    Laboured against boredom,
    Face scanned face and moved inwards
    Voices lapsed with quiet strain.

Just for a while, a sea lake
Touched a red fox's paw, washing imperceptibly,

Grain by grain,
The sea birds perched around
Their marriage bed, one grass island
Or a tree-lined shore

We rocked towards evening.

POEMS SELECTED
FROM
'THE SONG OF GOWER'

There was no time
Not when I leapt from a bent branch
And sprang skywards,
Nor when I listened to dawn sounds

I ran through minutes

As a mountain stream
Sculptures her stone-bed
careless in her clean power
And free.

Time grew when I piled stones
And made walls to hold me,
It split my days
And marked the night's hour

MOONCHILD

On top of the world away from the sea
Everything was silver:
On top of the sea away from the world
Everything was silver.

She saw moonlight on the cliffs
As he saw shadows,
And the moon made shadows change shape

He said she was made of moonlight
And could not understand:
She said the shadows were too dark
And they had no substance . . .

But they lay in the bright night together.

MOON CHANGES

The white flame has moved across the bay:
Last month it caught the headland, crooking
A light finger over the far shore,
But now it is closer and burns,
White manganese, flaring silently:
Its brightness wounds
All dreams shrivel in searing blaze.

GOWER CLIFFS

I will walk through the gorse,
Tasting the wine-soaked Summer'
Clothe myself in thorned gold,
Walking with time-honeyed
Bitterness.

Then I will remember
When tall cliffs, in bright banners
Were clothed, woven with sun thread;
And grass was thick
Where sea birds made a stairway.

WILD PONIES OVER HEATHERSLADE

Shimmering air, nothing but heat and space
Empties from distant azure over common;
Ponies, carved in chestnut and dappled grey,
Shining in summer coats with mane suncombed,
Stand, monolithic, against dazzling horizon.

Unconquered eyes stare bright, reflecting sun,
Uncompromising in the summer's heat:
Scorning shelter; wiser than centuries:
Ringed statues, silent, until the unhinged world
Begins with different storms and rain.

THE DOWN TRODDEN

We touch it always
knowing
it is our own

we handle defeat
feel the peaks and where
it dips
stroking
we wear it as a crown

it presses inwards
we smile as we trace
thorn-like points
and red staining

A THOUGHT

Let me remember
boulders, wet after the last tide;
as foam line withdraws

on this smooth day
waves, endless and listless, creep
levelling shore and sea
soothing a mercurial ocean
strands from bladder-wrack
lie in a last long rest

let me recall these days
when the sea is leaden.

EVENING AT PENDOWER

Leaning back into cooled sand
women talk by spiked dunes
long after television time.

Passing them we walk on
towards a sea sucked into shore.
Underfoot the ridged beach
is hard . . . still we move towards sea
submerged by slit gold cloud;

Others will walk as we walk
on the beach; long after television time
new children will tread
the ridged sand

THE MARTYR'S GRAVE

My evening now is cool and damp
grass grows over paths and traps
between blades, rain beads;
A stone moulders out of earth
leaning sideways, near chippered path
from Church to Lych gate;

Your name is washed by weather, illegible;

In this churchyard, silence
arches over generations accelerating seasons,
until, spinning backwards
the clock stops on a Winter night
lit by Communion candle-glow.

I see the altar, carmine and curling flame;
yourself, first not knowing
part of the billowing surplice
already licked by the tasting pyre;
I see your eyes dilate

then, wrapped in your own blanket of flame,
the shining brass of the Cross,
red and flickering in some devil's dance
with searing light and shadow,
stamped the sign of Martyrs
over your body.

As a thin branch in burning heath
you crumbled, sparks turning outwards
your crimson memory
illuminating.

CLEAR MORNING

Each star stabbed
the universe and
someone said that stars
are made of all the stuff
that we are . . . if we could
glow in our own dark corners

Stars are not ringed with
politics and violence
as we are. If we could only have our dark . . .
the brilliance of our lives
might even be more light

So be content that stars
are as we are.

THE HARVEST FAILED

No light
danced on the flying cloud
darkened by harvest tears

killed grass
lay slow mouldering
pungent as it recedes

evening
distraught harvesters remain inert
Winter's fodder lay to waste

gnarled hands lifted and sifted
no golden sheaves
dry and whispering

no June grass in January.

DO NOT REMIND HER

How could she not be garrulous
If one considers years
And her remembered laughter,
Many trials endured

Time is an inevitable stalker
There is much lessening
Of witnesses . . . no audience . . .
Few will arugue and less
Will concur

As for herself she deprecates
Some accuse with haste
Of nostalgia

Yet what memories!

CHRYSANTHEMUMS

Look! She sits in the kitchen,
Dark hair stranding puzzled face,
Lids slanting, almost pleased
At holding court, forgetting a moment,
Until unveiled eyes flicker on damp hands
Clutching handkerchiefs like flags
And linger on sombre Chrysanthemums
Before the tears

But this is it! He's gone;
This is why all these people
Blacken the road to the cemetery
And cars crawl like hearses
Down High Street.

They tell me they were close
He and his wife, they danced
Always together on Saturday nights
There were no barriers between them,
No embarrassment
Like wondering if people thought them soft

The Chrysanthemums crash against the wall
Scented undertakers. Large for sorrow.

No one knows me in this crowd
Of friends and hushed gossip
Though I explained exactly who I am
And sit making conversation
Conscious every word lances the silence
Which will melt I know
When I have gone.

Then I remember his smile
Proved a moderate courtesy
And understand her sadness.
Too late! My pity is thinned,
All warmth contained in coffin pride,
If she could only know
I envy her, her nailed grief,
The humility of widowhood;

Her vulnerability to all the love
    Spreading as blooms around the walls.

EXTRA-MURAL
RELATIONSHIP

He is quite affable

    complaisant and mindful
    of our years.
    He aims to draw
    in pungent phrases
    thoughts filed before fax
    and floppy discs
    made memory painless.

Not one young face here

    only worn minds
    unused to pandering
    and old eyes which
    watch with misgiving
    print on rainbow sheets
    computer compositions.

Uniformed in tweed,
chalk impregnated,
arm stretches to blackboard,
scrapes a word . . . two words . . .

    We think of bodies in small chairs,
    he thinks of bodies;
    we see a swallow-dip
    glance at watch,
    a measuring expression
    and he surveys
    ancient children.

REFELECTIONS

There should be children by this stream
Breached by thorned brambles, browned
By July sun and swept by October gales
To remain for ever,
Only bubbling froth creates laughter

Through edging grass my feet stumble
I clutch my stick . . . its carved groove
Comforts my grip
Eyes absorbing . . .
But eyes should wonder
Not notch another season's reckoning

Always the same
Yet I sense an emptiness,
A panic . . . I must not be the last
To feel the breath of winter.

AFTER THE STORM

I stared at a buffeted world
The storm which had screamed all night
Through hanging wires and whitened,
Torn trees was spent

Now dawn, blind windows cleared,
Leaves lay on concrete,
Concrete, washed and clean, smelling
Of moss

Grass leant and water beaded each blade
Above the fenny landscape
Grass shone

My boy pulled on an anorak
Slammed after me; we savoured
Calm after a night's fear

His rubber boot kicked the land
Shaved branches lay as they were blown
Last leaves were dead

He wondered at their red number
'as if the trees have bled'.

Each year the first storm rants,
Blusters more fiercely,

    'when will we be safe?'

I had to shake my head,
'Each time we learn some things must be
yet they will pass.'

'when will we know?'

the small boy's coat flapped
in the infant wind
which followed the storm,

I pointed to a bared branch,
Birds twittered into wet light,
Flew over a wooden shed,
Dug into a damp earth for food:

'Watch for the birds,' I said.

WARTIME CHAT-UP
ON THE FALMOUTH FERRY

Did you see the fish with silver stripes
and a blue tiara

swimming through the loop in a
Lobster's claw

That's the Captain's supper, he'll cook
it in the white steam foam from
the bow.

He says that because his wife is a mermaid
he never admits to liking fish.

That's the flip flap sound we heard
behind the ropes in the stern, Marina
with her fish tail under an apron

she's learning the floral dance for the
carnival . . . one . . . two . . . three . . . hop on a fish tail

he'll not let her go
that's not fair . . . she's learnt to hop.

THE FARMER'S WIFE

Tacking downwards
The minute hand
On the grandfather clock races –
Gaining seconds,
Yet the sound is the same . . .

You will listen
Without heed as time measures,
For outside the sun
Gains the hill's shoulder
And sounds of milk churns clash;

A tractor throbs
And Gwyn has moved to Ty'n y Cwm
To bring the hay;
Elfed saws wood
David is intent as he watches;

Cows move in the top field
David's fingers trace
A worn peg in the stable door;
There is quiet;

And then you rise,
Pushing a paper aside
With all the world's news;
You gather meat
From broth and peel potatoes:

You eyes look always
Seeing the sweat soaked clothes;
The golden glare
Of summer's harvest.

FOR *ALOUETTA* . . . ONE OF
THE GALLANT FLEET

He looked away from a wooded edge
Of river where lines of 'yuppie' yachts
Raised from the salt-stained shingle
(lest Cornish rain should soil
those elegant designer beams)

he then recalled the night
in summer time when, on a placid Fal
he felt his battered boards,
caressed the scars of bullets
gained when this small boat chugged

through white-tipped channel lane
Dunkirk ! 'Mission just to save'
and *Alouetta*'s curved and sharpened
bow cut through the grey sea waves
'if ever a boat had heart'.

And on that shingle lined with yachts,
Waiting for easy seas,
This little boat should lie alone,
A monument , saluting
An armada which did not fail.

THE AFTERMATH

A notebook amongst his effects
Fastened in sealed cover
Official and intimate

A Garden of Gethsemane
Why and when soldier tourist?
Mentioning names of girls:

Sleeping the ex-soldier cried
Un-recognising safe bed,
Hospital and fine white sheets . . .

An Oriental landscape his
Bamboo and sizzling tin roof
Flicking with stick and boots

Or worse . . . his torment still
Inflicted in his mind's video:

An airman, eagle-eyed
By day and feared, silent, cold;
Under night's cover, his mangled hand
Reaching out and words

Tumbling, incoherent . . . terror
And stench and threatened
Loss of love.

Records playing our songs
We danced in smoky village halls
White cliffs and Johnny's bed

Poppies scatter on our heads
Settling . . . blood around our shoes.

THE NIGHT'S SILENCE

Each room is empty
I am alone to dream
or gather old conversations

see lost faces . . . a creak
on the stairs . . . maybe the wind

but the creak has a purpose
a walk from the past
into new life

but all sounds in this house
are friendly . . . lovers' steps
and I also love

here I can feel all those
who surround me
and know good company.

TO WRITE IN RETROSPECT

'I was there' you write . . .
I can believe your fear and feel
oppression as you breathe
the need to draw in deep cool air
each window open,
though the room, your prison grows tight.

Farmers soaked, crossing
the yard towards the milking shed
ploughing a field . . . boots
heavy in troughs of freezing mud
each journey needed for
God cannot protect each lamb.

You returned from war
leaving mates strung on barbs
or stranded on Dunkirk sand
still as battles raged on bridge twisted
metal and cold or stand behind
electric fence in searchlight glare

you should have written . . .
not these scribes who draw
false heroics from lives
sentiment cannot be second hand.

HIGH CROSS REVISITED

Modernisation in a Cornish city.

Cobbles glistened
Misted like old eyes
which stare into memory.

To see once more
tough ponies clattering and
old carts rattling

towards ramshackle Pydar

The skyline shocked as
shocks a stripped octogenarian
in a disco

blue nothingness
the same a summer visitor
sees when devouring

our sea and yellow sand

which weaves a cloak
to hide our undertows
and sinuous veins of ore

brash architect
who dared erase
our known horizon

which etched its slow pattern

to draw new lines which must fail
to compensate
for crumbled stone and dust.

This new world's edge
so planed and sharp
devoid of corners to hold dreams

or fantasies.

CONSULT YOUR LOCAL OFFICE

Remember when the masts of ships were seen
from Lemon Street and mud flats
where the car park stands?

    No thoughts, count, keep the computer posted,
    switch off such obstructive dreams:

smell of hot bread or peeled apples
in narrowed kitchen warmth;
a deflective scent from wet hedge?

    such thoughts steal through memory
    they are not relevant to the day:

subversions not expected,
like laughter which mocked us out of childhood?

work by control, the time gauge
is geared for longer leisure,

    RELAX . . . THE Minister of Pleasure
    has got the whole thing taped:

is all this sentiment drowned
locked under filled river-beds?

    SEE THE WHITE PAPER, NOW AVAILABLE.

DARBY AND JOAN

He says 'Where are you going?'
and I answer, 'anywhere,
out of range of criticism
or loud anger and the crusted dream
which was love'.

I say, 'I can do that thing
or lift this, without rancour or wrangling
which sets each nerve jangling'
but words do not get through,
the rough barnacles covering
our frail brown love.

He says, 'Wait a minute,
I cannot rush,' and when he fails
he blames his eyes . . . the cataract occludes
the years when all was seen so fair:
there were winters and hot summers and mostly
green, plump-bedded Spring times.

JERICHO

He built a city with white walls and streets
between tall houses; banked with fountains
and theatres,
he made a castle and was repaid,
it was his own creation.

He built with satisfaction . . . yet
he could tumble, pushing his pile of rubble,
fingers crushing stones and spilling,
sensuously, as a child stirs sand
on beaches.

He made something tangible
to please more in devastation.

lonely morning star
bright in this December dawn
small gleam in the dark

NIGHT MENACE

An owl hooted in the moon dark,
a Harrier's call descant to sounds
of a vixen or the chained farm dog;

a perfect pitch, a tune-forked warning
beasts fretted to the lichened bough.

too-whoo, to-whoo, drawn music and
silent feathered power of wings
swept through woodland path and barn:

outside, mauve red, the glow was subdued,
frozen haze and the moon was wan:

menacing was star-sparked darkness
in the crunch of evening . . . winter trees
lay stark and brittle in the not-yet frost;

through moonlight and petrified branches
for sometime kindling, the owl still cried.

SATURDAY NIGHT
IN AUGUST

August and Saturday night
a rush of vibrant colour,
forget the season's silage;
fields spread with white cotton,
cotton to blazon bare shoulders;

soft cotton with Harlem patterns
and the sun, exploding diffuses
this summer-tinted lane,
tarry smells pervade

jazz and Southern Comfort,
cars drive for out of town
and thread a rural haze,
drinks on trestles later;

tipped glasses
Mint Julep and the Rosebay Willow,
careless splashes,
beer and body language;

new age conversation,
maybe . . . but who needs talk,
a slit skirt, long as a gipsy's, sways

laughter and laziness,
a woman leaning over rails,
dark eyes challenging

daring the sun to dip.

MORNING COFFEE
IN THE WHITE HART

He said 'in the Post
They let me know
I've got more Pension . . .'

'Aw,' said the other
pouring his morning coffee
'It's all to do with the . . .'

a third chipped in
'with the cost of living
like when the rates went up

and everything else this year,'
'Why don't they say. . .?'
And they sipped their coffee.

Next they mentioned how
Vicious were mosquito bites
in Portugal.

A LAST APPRAISAL

The land was no longer his
Although for years he ploughed
And tilled, milked his cattle
Twice a day and when the trees
Spread with wild abandon
He would prune and plant elsewhere

He knew when north winds
Battered walls and when the snows
Fell in piles, still glittering
As white sun struck their gold,
Where cattle stood and basked,
Knew this was his farewell walk.

He touched a stone and stroked a flower
And when he reached a place
V-shaped with trees to shade;
Where mares with foals were quick
To gather against all winds,
He whispered his good-bye.

The peace which must have been the breath
Of such content . . . when with jaws slack
And hind leg curved, his lovely herd
Had dreamt or slept, secure
Against a sting of flies or blast of wind
Their spirit now returned as if

To comfort his despair.

ONCE AN ACORN

It is unfinished
Though days of growth have passed
Years when my feet burrowed
Through woodland mulch
Deep, to the secret earth
And stretched, dinosaur claws
Making secure and drawing sustenance.

Then each leaf was spread
In the changing light of seasons
Sacrificing life each Autumn
An ancient pagan rite
Promising renewal
'oh those proud centuries
when I could round and reach'

holding my ams as branches
hold the world

now living senses
remembered still have mellowed
I can no longer feel the wind
Yet your fingers brush my surface
And I am silk beneath your touch,
I gleam and breathe;
Your hand must open

Soft the feel of palms
Which absorb the primal warmth

And I am strong, those years spent in tidal mud
Were a fierce tribal test
And I repaid with strength,
I know the soft caress
Of arms which lean across me;
I hear the gossip of the years . . .
I bear silver treasures and set fair
A crystal brilliance,
Glasses filled with wine might toast
My own resilience.

Yet set me near the window
And let the sun reflect
The spirit of light upon
My age scored boards

A golden glow bright with summer
is my own benefaction.

CRY OF THE CURLEW

Clarity of sky
Emphasising moon's brilliance
It shames the shadows

These are the small hours
Outside walls there is silence
Inside the clocks tick

Ices sparks in sunrise
The world is a wedding cake
Hand burns on white lace

Red sky in cold dawn
Cattle's breath spirals in barn
A world is ringed by cloud

I hear the curlew
Why is he always laughing?
He mocks the false spring

White-wash on cow shed
All spring work is completed
obliteration

FAN IS DEAD

The scoured lane is empty
and red rimmed windows on cream building
this day, add to the mourning;
there is silence and the tumbled welcome
which poured and flowed
through the guttered hollow
is stemmed.

'Only a bitch' you say,
adding in stolid grief; 'but a good one';
forgetting, our eyes search a while
for the lithe form, black white, which leapt
as high as the heart sings over fields
to call in heifers or to welcome;
the honest muzzle lying as warm
as all love against a knee.

So Sylen dons her drapes
This February day and weeps
And I shall search through
Barbed banks and where the gorse
Tufts on thin soil and see
Fan wait, head pointing in the wind;
Eyes bright as sunlight.